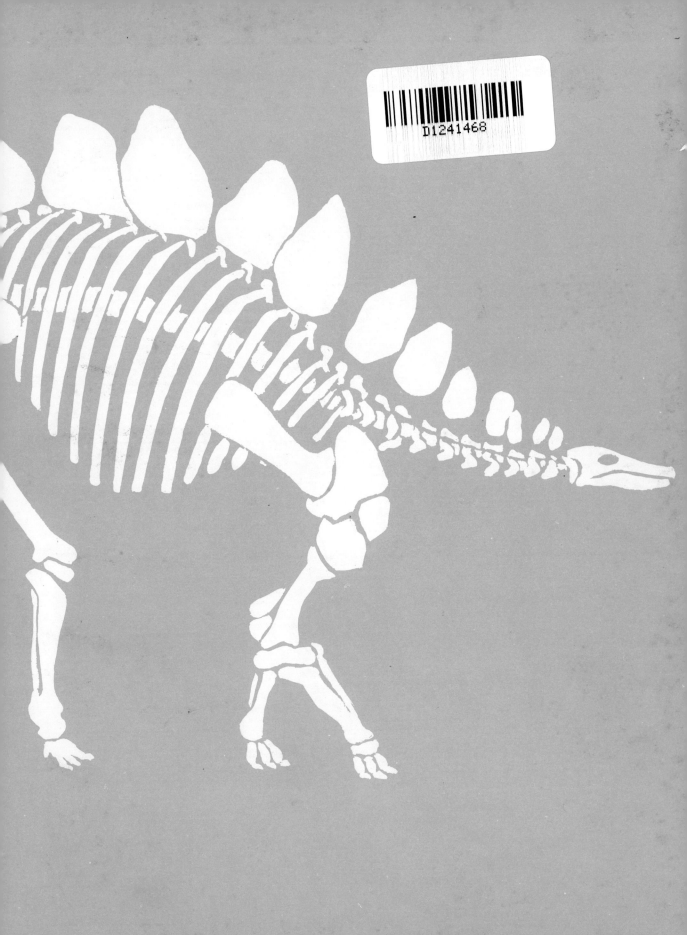

A

McGraw-Hill Book Company   NEW YORK • TORONTO • LONDON • SYDNEY

DOZEN
DINOSAURS

by Richard Armour

Paul Galdone drew the pictures

Also by Richard Armour
with pictures by Paul Galdone

The Year Santa Went Modern
The Adventures of Egbert the Easter Egg
Animals on the Ceiling
Odd Old Mammals

ACKNOWLEDGMENTS

For advice and encouragement I am grateful to my friend, Raymond M. Alf, paleontologist and inspiring teacher at the Webb School of California, and to the always helpful members of the Department of Geology at Pomona College.

A Children's Choice Book Club Edition

Two hundred million years ago
In what is now Wyoming,
Midst Mesozoic jungle swamps
The dinosaurs were roaming.

Some dinosaurs were lizardlike,
Still others crocodilian,
With names like Protoceratops
Instead of Fred or Lillian.

Some fed upon the leafy plants
That grew along the shore,
While some ate those who ate the plants,
Then looked around for more.

Some walked upon all fours, as you'd
Expect of such a beast.
Some walked two-legged, like a man.
There all resemblance ceased.

A few were small as dog or cat,
　　But most were quite enormous.
Take BRONTOSAURUS, eighty feet
　　In length, as books inform us.

So big was Brontosaurus that
　　One brain would not suffice.
Besides the wee one in his head
　　He had, and this was nice,

Another brain, or bunch of nerves,
　　Placed rather near the rear
That doubtless had the duties of
　　Assistant engineer.

Despite his size, his skin was soft,
　　His mouth was thin and weak,
And nothing much protected him
　　From tooth or claw or beak.

4

bron-toe-SAW-rus

So Brontosaurus never strayed
    Far from the water's edge.
With peglike teeth he dined all day
    On grassy plants and sedge.

And when an enemy drew near,
    This Brontosaurus slid
Into the water hurriedly,
    And there he wisely hid.

Sometimes, in fact, he stayed beneath
    The surface for so long
His friends would wonder if perhaps
    His breathing had gone wrong.

Then up he'd pop, and just in time
    To save himself from drowning,
And everyone would be relieved
    And say, "He's only clowning."

Who was this enemy he feared?
　　Why was it that he fled him?
Well, it was ALLOSAURUS, and
　　He had a right to dread him.

For Allosaurus, huge and high,
　　On two hind feet went zipping.
His toes were tipped with hooklike nails
　　That badly needed clipping.

His bite was very special too.
　　His jaws were chomping whizzers.
His lower teeth and uppers worked
　　Much like the blades of scissors.

8

al-o-SAW-rus

He munched and crunched and crunched and munched
    With monstrous appetite,
And those who fled him did not wish
    A bit to be a bite.

"Look out, look out for Allosaur—!"
    Each creature warned his friend.
Should any stumble as they ran,
    Too bad—that was the end.

Well built for nibbling leaves of trees
    And also for a laugh,
BRACHIOSAURUS we might call
    A dinosaur-giraffe.

On long front legs, with lifted neck,
    The landscape he surveyed.
You might well wish that you were he
    When watching a parade.

Since seasons all were sticky hot,
    Spring, summer, winter, autumn,
He mostly stayed in marsh or lake,
    His big feet on the bottom.

And yet his little ostrich head
    Stuck out above the surface
So he could take a look around.
    (Not seeing made him nervous.)

How lucky that his nose was not
    Placed in our nose's place
But on the tiptop of his head
    And well above his face.

With built-in snorkel he could breathe
    Yet stay down safe and cool.
He may look rather odd to you,
    But please, no ridicule.

ORNITHOLESTES liked dry land,
　　This dainty, darting thing,
Much like a bird except for lack
　　Of feathers and of wing.

Although he couldn't fly, he fled
　　Upon his two quick feet
And in the jungle thicket hid
　　From those that sought his meat,

Like Allosaurus, always starved,
　　That creature great and grim,
Who would have opened wide his mouth
　　And made one bite of him.

Ornitholestes put his trust
　　Upon a speedy getaway.
And if you were so small and shy,
　　Could *you* think of a better way?

He too, however, had to eat.
　　No food was on his shelf.
And so he fed on any creature
　　Smaller than himself.

For instance Archaeopteryx,
    An early bird indeed,
And reptiles, insects, anything
    That served his stomach's need.

But then, had he not grabbed them up
    And chewed and gulped his fill,
They would no doubt have done the same
    To creatures smaller still.

Some saved their hides by hiding in
    The water, some by running.
But STEGOSAURUS saved his skin
    With skin. How's that for cunning?

His outsides kept his insides in
    With many boltlike bumps.
Upon his back were rows of plates,
    Points up, unpleasant humps.

Though he outweighed an elephant,
    His brain was walnut size.
Head down, he clumped through palms and ferns.
    He won no beauty prize.

steg-o-SAW-rus

In Colorado and Wyoming,
   In fact throughout the land,
Had you lived then, you might have seen
   His footprints in the sand.

Attacked, he'd flail his tail and say,
   "Take that!" with grumpy grunts,
And with four handy, dandy spikes
   Punch four holes all at once.

If Stegosaurus had few friends
   And lacked the social knack,
One thing was sure: he made it hard
   To pat him on the back.

Now let us leave Jurassic times
  And come to times Cretaceous,
When dinosaurs, though different,
  Were not a lot more gracious.

Back then, when Kansas was a sea,
  The sky was filled, they say,
With birdlike beasts about as large
  As many planes today.

PTERANODON, for instance, soared
  In swooping, gliding flight.
So little did he flap his wings,
  He looked more like a kite.

His hands were fastened to his wings,
   Or wings, perhaps, to hands,
And not with rope or wire or tape
   Or glue or rubber bands.

Three fingers, though, stuck out in front,
   Well made to grab and hold,
But rather rough and bony things
   For shaking hands, we're told.

His head was narrow, hammer shaped,
   All bone, with little fat on.
A head like this it would be hard
   To keep a cap or hat on.

His eyes were large, for sighting fish,
   Which, since his mouth was toothless,
He swallowed still alive and whole.
   Fish thought him rather ruthless.

Pteranodon looked like a kite,
   I've said. Now tell me, friend,
How would you like to hold the string—
   If he were at the end?

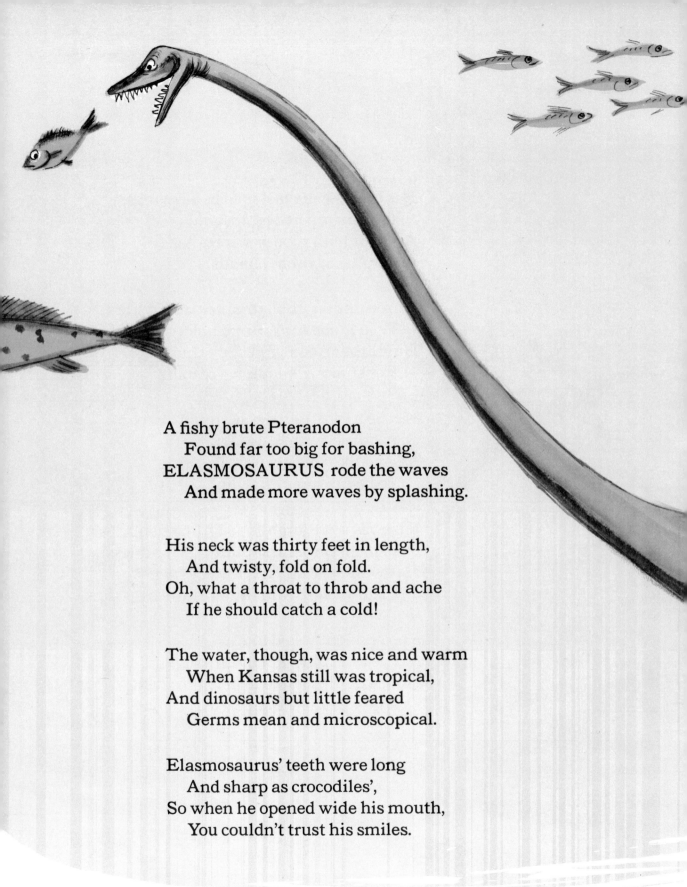

A fishy brute Pteranodon
   Found far too big for bashing,
ELASMOSAURUS rode the waves
   And made more waves by splashing.

His neck was thirty feet in length,
   And twisty, fold on fold.
Oh, what a throat to throb and ache
   If he should catch a cold!

The water, though, was nice and warm
   When Kansas still was tropical,
And dinosaurs but little feared
   Germs mean and microscopical.

Elasmosaurus' teeth were long
   And sharp as crocodiles',
So when he opened wide his mouth,
   You couldn't trust his smiles.

His body was a stubby sort,
    His skin like polished leather.
He looked as though a snake and fish
    Were somehow stuck together.

His fins he doubtless used for oars.
    His tail was like a rudder.
Small fish who saw him steer their way
    Would sigh, "Oh, my!" and shudder.

The sea today has sharks and such
    Of which one must beware,
But swimmers should rejoice there's no
    Elasmosaurus there.

e-laz-mo-SAW-rus

Among the later dinosaurs
    Though not the largest, strongest,
PACHYCEPHALOSAURUS had
    The name that was the longest.

Yet he had more than syllables,
    As you may well suppose.
He had great knobs upon his cheeks
    And spikes upon his nose.

Ten inches thick, atop his head,
    A bump of bone projected.
By this his brain, though hardly worth
    Protecting, was protected.

No claw or tooth, no tree that fell
    Upon his head kerwhacky,
Could crack or crease or jar or scar
    That stony part of Paky.

And so he nibbled plants in peace
    And lived untroubled days.
Sometimes, in fact, as Paky proved,
    To be a bonehead pays.

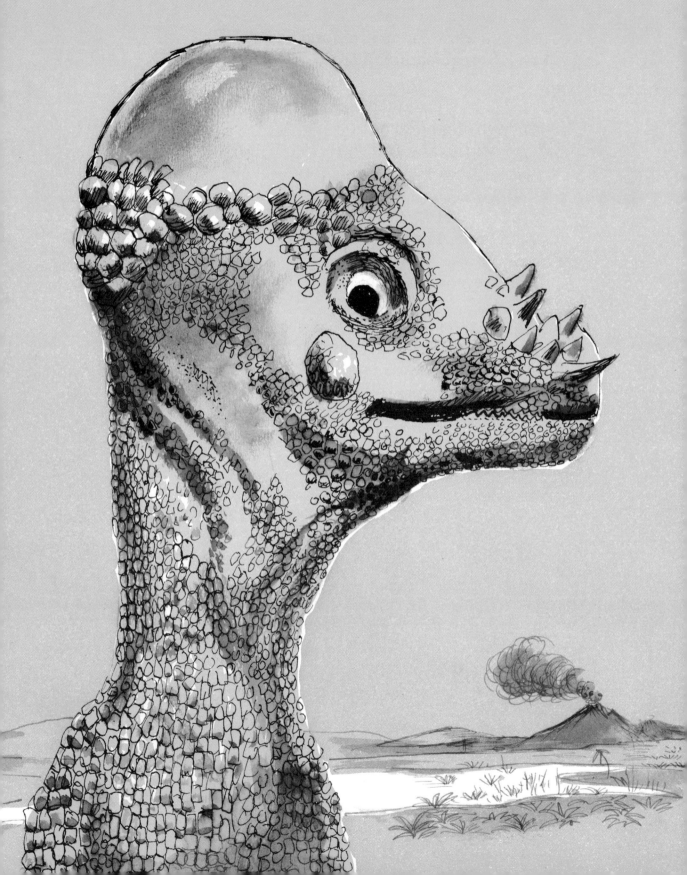

pak-i-SEF-a-lo-SAW-rus

Though many million years had passed
    Since dinosaurs appeared,
There still were creatures big and bad
    That lesser creatures feared.

So dinosaurs still needed horns
    And shields and some bravado
While lazing in and grazing in
    Cretaceous Colorado.

TRICERATOPS was well equipped
    With horns. His numbered three,
One on his nose's tip and two
    Where eyebrows ought to be.

And as for shields, to shield his neck
    From those who tried to grab it
He had a fancy bony frill
    He wore from force of habit.

Still stranger was his birdy beak
    That made him seem a parrot.
Few dared to call him Polly, though,
    Or offer him a carrot.

A third of him, about, was head.
    It seemed more than he needed.
It measured seven feet in length.
    Who had a big head? He did.

An enemy might well sneak up
    And seize him from behind.
But should he choose to face his face—
    Well, he'd have lost his mind!

try-SER-a-tops

ANKYLOSAURUS, even more
   Encased in plates of bone,
Was like an Army heavy tank
   Or building made of stone

Or like a vault or like a fort
   With walls around the center.
Most took the hint. They did not need
   A sign that said, "Don't enter."

Besides, he had a sturdy tail
   With which he did his best
To club and drub and thereby snub
   An uninvited guest.

an-ki-lo-SAW-rus

Not made for speed, he never sped
    But slowly moved around
And grazed upon the greenery
    Where tasty plants were found.

Sometimes, perhaps, not looking up,
    His path he poorly guided.
Triceratops and he made quite
    A crash when they collided!

No harm was done. Their plates were thick.
    No dents at all, or barely.
Moreover, traffic being light,
    This happened very rarely.

What took the pleasure out of life
    For every living thing?
TYRANNOSAURUS REX. (The "rex"
    Means he was boss, or king.)

A tyrant was Tyrannosaurus,
    Forever seeking food.
The others, though they loved to chew,
    Weren't fond of being chewed.

So they retired when he came near,
    Behind a ginkgo tree
Or deep in water or inside
    Their outside armory.

Tyrannosaurus' jaws were traps
    Of steel, they were so strong.
His mouth was full of jagged teeth
    At least six inches long.

His forelegs might seem tiny things,
    More like a dog's, indeed.
His hind legs, though, were quite enough
    For any leggy need.

In fact he had not only claws
    Upon his toes to grip with
But on each ankle, in the rear,
    An extra claw to rip with.

tye-RAN-o-SAW-rus

And so this tyrant rex made wrecks
Of beasts both fatter, thinner.
He grabbed them firmly with his teeth
And hauled them off for dinner.

His head held high, he looked afar,
　　And if he chanced to meet you,
He'd say, politely, "Hello, friend.
　　How are you? Pleased to eat you."

We come at last to TRACHODON,
   Who, ducklike in the face,
Seemed very little like a duck
   In any other place

Except for webbing on his feet,
   For wings and such he lacked.
He may perhaps have waddled some—
   I doubt he ever quacked.

This Trachodon stayed in or near
   The water all the time.
With ever-eager outstretched bill
   He slip-slopped through the slime.

He searched, you see, for tender slugs
   And cuttlefish and crabs,
All which he ate, along with plants,
   In gulps and dibs and dabs.

He lived in both the East and West
   But liked what's now New Jersey,
In those days mostly ponds and streams,
   All flowery and furzy.

Of dinosaurs he lasted last,
   But he too now is gone.
If what you see looks like a duck,
   It isn't Trachodon.

TRAKE-o-don

What made the dinosaurs die out
    Despite their strength and size?
Some blame it on their little brains
    And lack of enterprise.

For instance, when the climate cooled
    And chilled them to their throats,
They never thought of underwear
    Or gloves and overcoats.

And when it turned from moist to dry
    And swamps began to fail,
They brought no water in by pipe
    Or aqueduct or pail.

Give thought, then, to the dinosaurs,
    Whom one no longer dreads.
They used their teeth and used their claws
    But didn't use their heads.

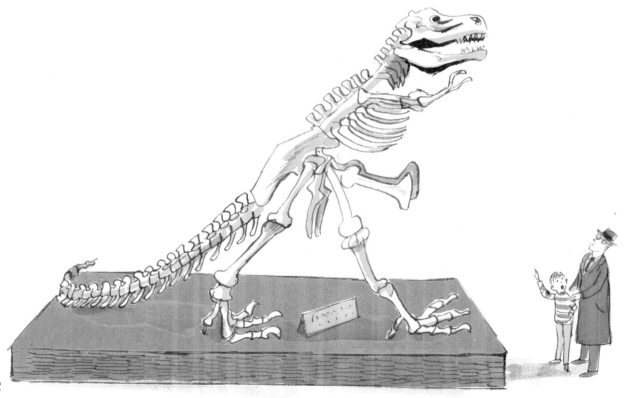

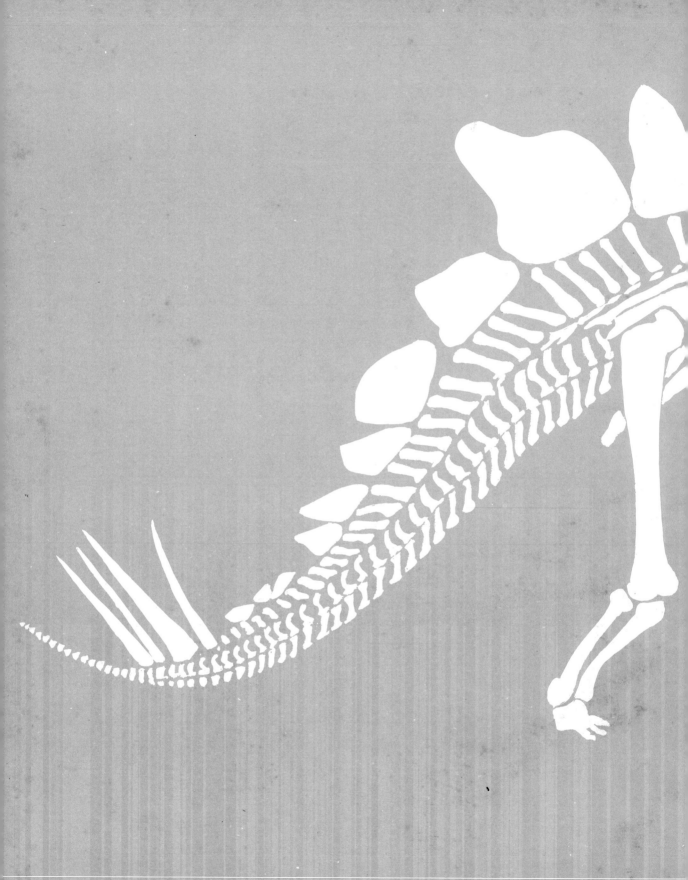